An Absence of, An Earnest

a poem by

James Maynard

Finishing Line Press
Georgetown, Kentucky

An Absence of, An Earnest

Publisher: Leah Maines

Editor: Christen Kincaid

Cover Art: "Dancers", by Adam Bacher, www.conspiracyofravens.com

Author Photo: Susannah Maynard

Cover Design: Elizabeth Maines McCleavy

Printed in the USA on acid-free paper.
Order online: www.finishinglinepress.com
also available on amazon.com

Author inquiries and mail orders:
Finishing Line Press
P. O. Box 1626
Georgetown, Kentucky 40324
U. S. A.

—for Sinta

"Why do people not think, when they are grown up, as I do when I'm young?"

"Oh dear," said Merlyn. "You are making me feel confused. Suppose you wait till you are grown up and know the reason?"
~ T.H. White

The living, writers especially, are terrible projectionists.
I hate the way they use the dead.
~ Adrienne Rich

i.

Ten years.   So write a song
To sing the slow train home.

About the possum and the owl,
Or the badger and the bear,

Time was when I was a young man wild
Husky and sinning in the fresh mountain air.

Fear came later. The sapling grew to such a height
Some limbs began to die. Still, says I,

"I'm alright—*ja*,   *ja oui*,   *oui*,
Sí, *sí*—the ship's weathered

But there's strong wood, and the crew's
Not so rich as they'd wish to be."

Like a crow drops a walnut from a certain height,
Careful to fall as the walnut falls,

This poem I'm meant to write, ten years
To crack its contents in the sudden white

Where the crow had perched—
As raindrops pock the half-baked clay

Raising the aroma of wet earth,
This poem rises from a name, and from a distance

An
Absence

Splashes back to mind. Gabriel. Wait.
The scar is a clean scar.

+

In the mornings I open my book
of collective nouns and read aloud,

A lock of hair. Skirl of pipers. A tilt of windmills. Clew of worms.

I discover a multitude of husbands is,
Like an impatience of wives, meant

To *knock not the husband*
But the wife, inferring harlotry and pecking

Hens. For the poet there's a choice
Of a meter, an obscurity and

(
My favorite
For its guttural reverb
)

A gang.
My life in the throat in the throat like a cradle

The smoke from our cigarettes rise
Into the clear-cold night.

We watch the girls run up from the river,
Their skirts damp & clinging where they'd waded in.

And follow the snake of road to the canyon's rim,
We write like a couple of stone clouds
Has a cool crooned limp—

Or we trundle through the train yard
To the north side cemetery.

(
A suit of bodies, an assortment
Of graves.
)

When DEATH was not a horror but a word
We set as children's blocks
On top of blocks, cathedral-spired.

Until on an orange extension cord
You hung no sound,

No air for sound, and no one there
To make a violence of the air,

While you strangled and expired.

+

From the window by my writing desk,
In the cobalt heat my wife steps through

The front yard. Swaying her hips
To Bob Marley in faded blue jeans she picks
Strawberries ripe from the July sun

Inside our small, abundant patch.
Then she sees me. From behind the shades

In the clutter of my little desk,
She sees me and lifts her hands, kitchen scissors
Waving through the air.

And I wave back. Connections, made.

\+

In the night I think of the dead, angrily
I think of the dead,
Furiously I think of the dead.

+

And in the night—who was It—?
Who was It who spoke & sighed?

In the night there was more than silence,
While your father went dying room to room

The stuffyhot late July, horrible night,
Heavy in the heat below the drone of fans

The drone beneath the fans,
Prayer our bodies not betray us,
Pray pestilence never take us—

Dark night
Hot as hell

So hot the piano strings—hum—Who's there?
Too dark for shadows, but for shapes in shadows

From the corner where you died.
Something moved.

+

And why ten years would call
For update, examination, redress

(
Why the turn of two digits
Should work in your bones a rattle
)

Perplexes me even if I sleep.

I am asleep,
And my wife so comfortably beside,

And out from the curtains
Gabriel walks,
Still his young twenty-one

—and when I rest now
My bones can be heard to creak

—and when I smoke now
My lungs can be heard to crack

—and Gabriel
Walks

As though nothing is easier
Than a second coming—

A stone sunk in the ground
Other stones gather to—

So although it's been years,
And you've been peaceful, remote,

An ever-present Silence projecting out,

I approach this benchmark listening more
Toward your grave

To hear your silence stir,

We're all more than hushed to hear you,
—Gabriel

And the wisdom you may have gained
By your overwhelming
     stupid
       death—

+

An absence of.   An earnest.   A

wasteofgrace

hanging   drowning   falling   of.

Or scare, or star, or singular   ity   Of

a   love

A returning A   scab of   A lingering A   body bag of

open   theRiver   let   theBlood   rush   down.

—suicides   —selfMortifiers   —finalists   —theSprung.

Re lease.

Laughter of.   A night.

A nearness.   Covenant.

Obscurity.

ii.

Before dawn I wake   *give me*

Some light

And reach for my bathrobe switch
The light—*lights!*

Above the stove,
And the dog

Padding along behind me,
For it is breakfasttime and I

Understand more of Claudius
Than Hamlet—

Lights!

Whiles the dog's collar rings
Whiles she shakes her sleep away,

Anchoring me again, huge reality,
On the cold kitchen linoleum I

Can find my footing, start
A day, sitting down at my little desk,

Opening my books *my fault*
Is past.

+

When you hanged in the basement, Gabriel,
You pressed out a wrinkle for me.
Your self-murder a flat iron smoothing away

The idea that loss *is*, so it cannot be
Recovered, conjugated, cherished—

But in the week following your death
I remember meeting a friend of yours,

She was excited to see you again, she said,
"When will Gabe be back?"

Those sweet September days in Missoula
When the morning air is careless mountain cold,

And warm by noon with smells of river stones
Drying on the banks, I think I told her

She should sit down, and
Somehow managed a sentence of sorts,

Some kind of phrasing to indicate
Gabriel won't *be*, then watching her account for loss,

What amounts to loss,
Watching instantly a hole becoming,
And the work the body does to fill it,

It was pretty that day, while she wept,
It was late summer, best time of year,

As the mountains wait for winter,
And streams fill up with leaves.

+

Ten years later my wife & I drive
Through Olympia, Washington,
On our way to see your dying father.

We stop for lunch at a brewery there,
In the shade of city birch, on a terrace

With boisterous & foul-mouthed men,
The sun a white light perched at the plate's edge,

As vireos hop their dusty way
On the hot & crumby brick—

I tell the story of the first year ahead of you,
When I was twenty-three and full of steam

I toured the world south of Monterey,
Met a girl in Morro Bay,
She took me to a bay leaf forest by the shore.

We picked the leaves from the trees
And snapped them in our hands, the semi-sweet scent

Lifting from the skin—

+

And between the trees, new-age patchouli kids

(
A trip of hippies
)

Bend backward on the nurse logs
Jawing on about the Interconnected

(
An instance of cosmos
)

And bending back to look
Through

(
An autumn of
)

Leaves and

(
A regret of
)

Limbs into

Sky,

(

)

I think, then,
I walked the edge of
A superficial happiness,

I think happiness
Was a state of self
Becoming unaccounted,

And grief the state
Of self redefined

To the world per se : and
Where grief had been

These opening chords & interludes
Of the last ten years—even now

Sharing a pint of beer,
In the nectar heat, July's disinterested air—

I am startled into happiness,
Sudden & sustained octaves ringing in the treble,

And I know it to be happiness
Inside the grief,

Sitting epicureal on a quiet dusty street,
Poised for the shock of my dying friend, your father—

iii.

Buried your dad in the grave
Beside your grave, we

Buried your dad
In the grave beside
Your grave, we

Stood beneath the slated sky
Inside the slate-gray rain.

Your grave was slate & silent.

We stood beside you in the rain,
Buried your dad in the grave be
Side your grave we

Stood you in the rain, under
Ground we understood and
Standing saw buried

Your dad in the grave
Beside your grave, Gabriel,

How could you—
Your dad

Standing beside your grave
Beneath a slated sky,
Inside the slate-gray rain, why—

Gabriel I repeat, why—
Gabriel—did we stand beside you to

Bury beside you we are all
Beside you to see your dad

Safe in the grave,
Safe in the ground beside your ground we

Carry these graves around we
Know where we lay we

Buried your body in the slate gray rain,
Your dad in the ground beside you

Safely in the ground beside you now
Safe in the ground he lays.

+

She opens the scissors when her fingers splay
To wave at me in my clutter,

(
A wheeze of joggers, I chant, a play of
Possums. Parliament of owls.
)

My wife, bright life in the sunlight
Beckons me outside,

Twisting in her faded jeans
To No Woman No Cry.

There is. Work. To do.
I can't live my life
In collective nouns

The garden needs tending, the cosmo blooms
Drying

Into star shaped seed clusters I have
To tend my small lot daily day

To day they say on this
Here
Earth—

+

So, a song :

> Possum took a bus
From Des Moines to Sacramento.
In January when the last Arctic wind
Scurries on the Rockies southern hind,
The bus broke down west of Colorado.
On the road to Vegas Possum played possum
By day, at night he followed the road
In the bare brush and by the light of cars.
Possum was something like a fugitive.
Owl followed at a distance. He could do that,
And sleep by day while Possum acted dead,
He was curious why Possum behaved so furtively,
And Owl always followed his curiosity.
So often did it conclude philosophically.
It was slow going in the barren Utah desert,
Cold at night, Possum made hasty progress
Which wore him down, expended his energy.
One evening Possum did not rise up.
Owl woke to wonder what new deception
Possum had in store by playing possum at night,
When it was time to move and keep out the cold,
But Possum did not stir, and Owl,
Sure an answer would be forthcoming soon,
Stayed perched in the nook of a juniper bough.
From night to day to night this Owl
Could not conceive that Death may take presence
Over the action, that a master of the artifice
Might submit to the singular. Owl kept watch
Until he froze and fossilized. Then, whether or not
Possum stirred and began to slink south,
With the hope of finding berries winter forgot,
Is something the Owl would never know.

+

GABRIEL

the self betrays the body, the body
betrays the self

GABRIEL

why won't you rise, as I do, daily?

GABRIEL

and sort through this human frailty,
the waking and the sleeping,

GABRIEL

the crow found dead on the doorstep

GABRIEL

if you complete your sentence we define the words

GABRIEL

and remodel the words into the bodies of our own

GABRIEL

so your shadow is more like me
my desires and my fears

GABRIEL

and the death you gave yourself year by year
erodes

GABRIEL

like water on the haphazard trails we cut

GABRIEL

in those mountains that were for us — joy!

GABRIEL

why is joy so hard to see, a lumbering boor
I have to cage to see?

GABRIEL

now that you're the angel, within the cosmic trust

GABRIEL

now that you're the cosmic dust—

GABRIEL

you can speak the answer, now.
step out from that shadow's oblivion

GABRIEL

give me some light—

+

Here, this earth. A race of, a world.

(

        I close my book of collective nouns

)

A bitterness of. A wonder why we fit.

(

        and step into the afternoon

)

Lives we strike. Pose we leave.

(

        and inside a cluster of purple salvia,
        errant cosmos bloom

)

The years we water, such filtered hopes.

(

        and picking blueberries with my wife,
        to freeze then jam them

)

The spring of youth, July of age

(

        to enjoy jam as noun and verb and—

        —we're jamming in the name of the Lord—

)

Absent friends. The earnest dream.

James Maynard received his M.F.A. in Poetry at the University of Alabama. He has been twice awarded the Alabama Prison Arts & Education fellowship. His poetry has appeared in many journals, online and in print, most recently *Permafrost, New Orleans Review,* and *Otis Nebula.* A chapbook, *Throwaways,* is available from his website. Currently residing in his hometown of Portland, Oregon, he puts in his time writing poetry, gardening, web development for his favorite bookstores or presses, and, most recently, fatherhood. Find more poems and information at jamesmaynardpoetry.com.